Look Up, Look Down!

Written by Catherine Baker
Illustrated by Sharon Harmer

Daisy

Zac

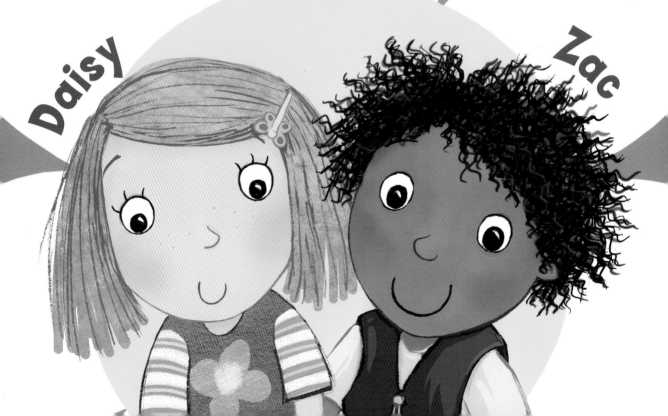

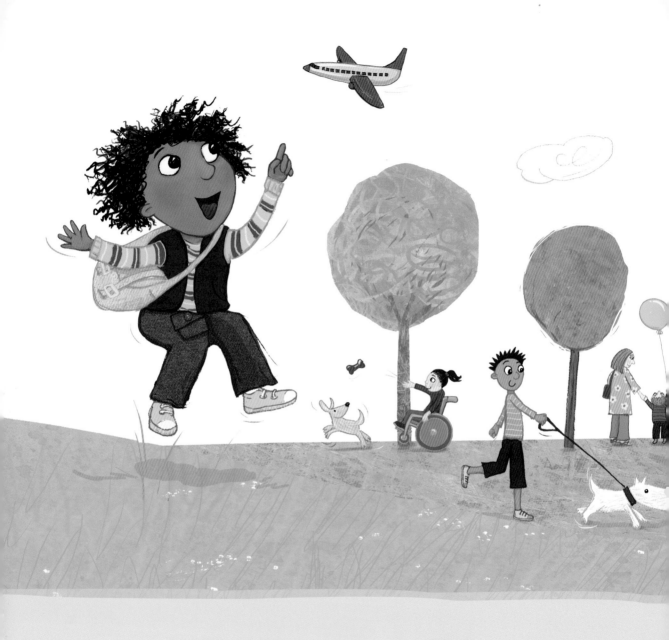

I can see a jet.

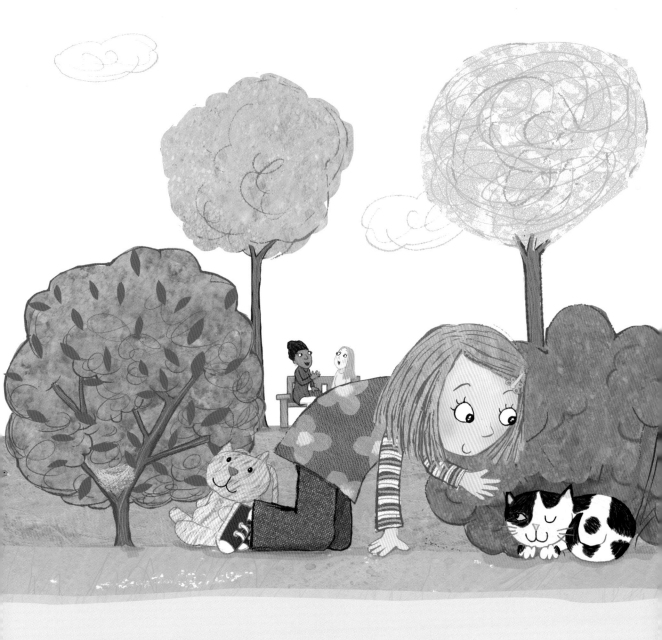

I can see a cat.

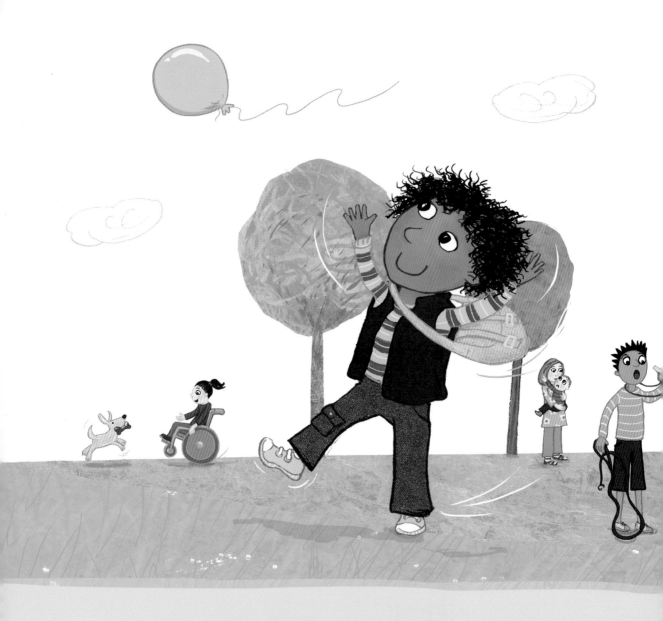

I can see a balloon.

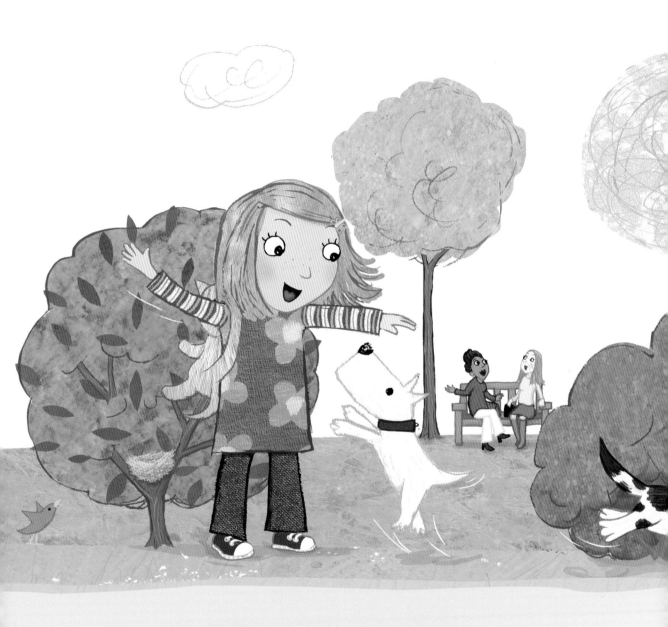

I can see a dog.

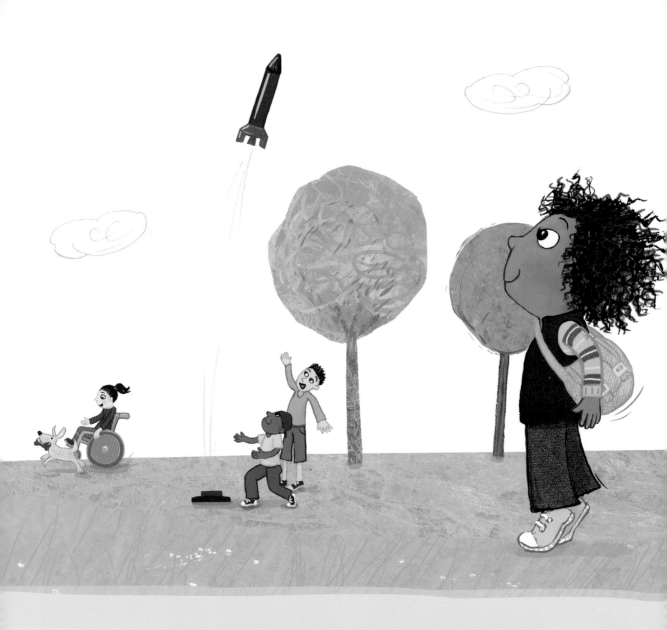

I can see a rocket.

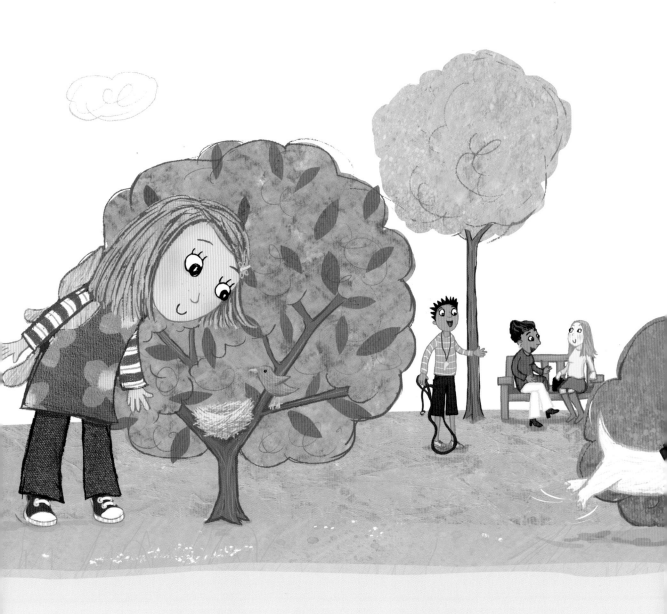

I can see a nest.

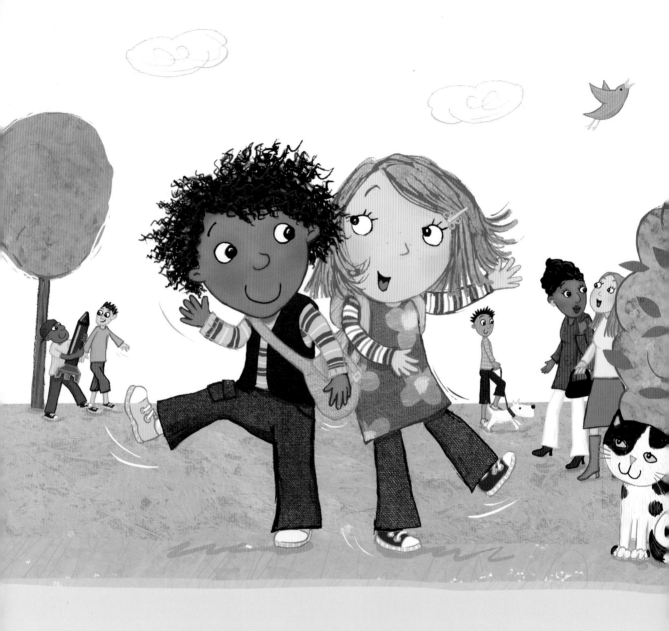

I did not see you!